THE POCKET MUSEUM
of NATURAL HISTORY

New Women's Voices Series, No. 184

poems by

MICHELE M MILLER

Finishing Line Press
Georgetown, Kentucky

THE POCKET MUSEUM
of NATURAL HISTORY

I only know I've walked the darkness wanting more than any Stonehenge to align with something bright.
—Albert Goldbarth

IN APPRECIATION

This book would not have been possible without the unflagging support of Becky
Byrkit, and the years of encouragement and generous spirits of Kelly Lewellyn, Stacey
Forbes, Barbara Sherman, Laura Issen, my mother and all three of my sisters. Gratitude
especially to Michael Mayes, who started this all.

Special thanks to Julie Speed for her inspiration and generous permission to use her
collage *Rosebud* on the cover.

For all of you, with love.

ACKNOWLEDGMENTS

Several of the poems in *The Pocket Museum of Natural History* were part of an
earlier manuscript chosen as runner-up by the National Poetry Series and the Kore
Press First Book Prize. Ten of them were selected as a submission for the Arizona
Commission on the Arts fellowship. The author is sincerely grateful for all, including
the below:

"Holy" and "Bee Litany" were short-listed for the FISH poetry prize judged by
    Billy Collins.
"Bee Litany" appeared in the *Paddock Review*.
"Snakes & Lovers" appeared in the *Blue Rock Review*.

Publisher: Leah Huete de Maines
Editor: Christen Kincaid
Cover Art: *Rosebud* by Julie Speed / www.juliespeed.com
Author Photo: Michele M Miller
Front Cover Design: Michele M Miller
Back Cover Design: Elizabeth Maines McCleavy

Order online: www.finishinglinepress.com
            also available on amazon.com

Author inquiries and mail orders:
Finishing Line Press
PO Box 1626
Georgetown, Kentucky 40324
USA

Contents

Confession of a Lepidopterist

O precious husk, O feral moonshine, O other-
worldly *odalisque* who wanes from abundant
abdomen to dust. *O Actias luna!* Pale green wings,
papery lamplit map of a darker time, limestone mimic
plucked mouthless from midnight's flower. You fossil
in my heart box, tombed in cotton, and summer rotates
back to summer in the crunch of thorax brooched
with a silver pin. O floating temptress, forgive me
this trespass: eye to eyespot, I was mesmerized.

Here, I offer my hand manifested as lover, one
who loves you beyond your brief life of lovemaking.
Caress me softly with both feathery stalks. Finger me
to shudder, O harem of filigreed clockwork feet.
O fixed architecture of hinge scissored from celadon
velvet and veins, it is I who am forever pinned: watcher
skewered to watched with each unboxing. Exquisite
corpse palmed like a wedding ring, your beauty
claws me open into willing prongs and I spiral, drunk
on the intimate emerald of you. O ephemeral jeweled
vestibule lifted heavenward on the deathbed
of my hand, I breathe, and it is you who tremble.

Bee Litany

Dancing
Dancing
Writing on air, rubbing out everything they write
Jerking their letters into knots, into tangles...
　　　　　—from "Gnat-Psalm" by Ted Hughes

When the bees creep at noontime
Bumbling over clover, drunk on summer
Slurring their alphabet of zees
Connoisseurring their stamen bouquets
Lurching high above mud-smudged slugs

Aeronautics cleanly absent of earth
Crystallize in hives of candied sun
Wings soothing in rhythm smooth white-hot
Palpitations of abdomens ripe with sting

Sleeping
Sleeping
Burning the branches black and yellow
Numbing fledglings with subcutaneous hum
Everybody everybody else's bell clapper, lullaby

Verb reverberates into noun: love

Not mumbling, not whispering, but tuning
Into the mother lode of all throb
Into the existential center contracting and expanding
Into the supernova of the next generation
Queen, belly full to bursting
Bursting she sings

That these are the seeds of the Sea of Sweetness
Larval motes in the eye of the bee-god
That they hear the stamens
Rejoicing in rain

And the morning meadow rejoicing
And the fields plowed to a brown gloss
Rejoicing in their fetal stalks

Olive buds plumped to bursting
And the torso of stump awaiting love
A heart
Rejoicing in the amber cells
The life dance vibrating in amber cells
Heart, antenna and lung and thorax
Feet and ichor and wing
Rising
Rising
In an accumulation of galaxy

And their terrible swift swords unsheathed, unceasing
Their tiny kaleidoscope eyes
Buttoning onto blossoms
Multiply petal exponentially into mandala
Pollen-laden legs combing the clover

O little Ambroses
Driven to live by your own hymns
Driving your adoration to death
You are the devils of sweet-tooth

And Beelzebub is a lowly pismire!
Your constellation swarms the entire sky
My eyes fly to heaven and are polished
My skin beads up in molecules of bonfire
My tongue shoves forward for communion

Your singing

Your singing

Hovers among my honeycombed bones
thrummed like strings

Wunderkammer

The great embalmers... kept their ingredients secret, but Ruysch apparently used some combination of wax, resin, talcum, and cinnabar pigment.
—Stephen Jay Gould

They are in Leiden, Netherlands, 1697. The tsar has come for Frederik Ruysch's cabinet of wonders, to add to his own collection of curiosities the numinous faces of infants bulging in rows of paraffin-sealed jars. This one someone's child pulled from a heap of rotten turnips and dung. This one hooked from a tangle of cattails in the harbor. Each head severed, washed with care, expertly prepared, then re-submerged. Ruysch's realistic elixir holds the subcutaneous filigree of veins plump, flushes the skin pink, one looks so close to moving it elicits a hitched breath from its admirer, Peter the Great.

He wants them all. So exquisite, an uncanny host of cherubim levitating in Ruysch's *liquid balsamicum*, monstrous bon-bons set on doilies the embalmer's daughter, Rachel, has sewn for them of her country's finest lace. From the shelf above his head, Peter reaches up and lifts down another one, smiles up into the face that, in falling forward, crushes its mouth against the glass between the giant's enormous hands. He can't help but kiss it, his royal lips smearing the glass.

4

Cumulonimbus

—for Kelly

In late summer Sonoran clouds
accumulate in fictions of shapes
enormous deities three times the height
of the peaks that bow below

giant white chrysanthemums of fireworks
our retinas have no time to burn into memory
a child's fairytale forest of cotton candy
processions of brides' hydrangeas in full bloom

we wish them into animals make boneless whales
and horses and dinosaurs who die and reincarnate
moment after moment after moment
never allowed to settle and rest

nebulae monoliths entirely similar
entirely separate until they are not
until they are siblings grown together
a smothering blanket of fleeced
darkness limned in twilight
lovely and sinister

these oracles predict rain
we long for but never believe will come
until water flashes and swarms
down every parched burrow
washes clean the tarantula and tortoise
digger bee and darkling beetle
ground squirrel and pack rat
pocket gopher kit fox hognose skunk
beaded lizard and spadefoot toad

mostly it is we who drown
arrogant in the flood rushing the dip
in the road we paved across an arroyo
that was blister and thirst
this morning and all last month
and months before that

this desert opens to live
we are transient bits of it the ground
uses to remake itself drop by drop

Holy

—for my grandfather

How can one O hold so much? This Monday even the potato
plump in its burrow is holy, and its siblings, stones cast out
by the plough, kneel at the edge of the measured rows and
are holy. The dirt, too, is holy, iced over and sewn with rotting

roots. Keeper of holiness to come, this fallow field invites
the breeze to pray in its naves, to bring alive what's left
of last season's wheat, beseech the clods for green shoots.
One pearly work-shirt button, suspended frozen in water

cupped by combine-tire track, glints in its singular sacredness.
Torn threads, empty of purpose, gesture from the flannel shirt
limp on its peg toward the old man still on the bed,
and this is a prayer. His horses in their stamped straw

whicker and snort at the numinous glamour thrown up
around them—where the barn window's light strikes dust
rising from their tail-whipped flanks, rumps crowned
with mote-made haloes, muzzles rimmed in warm

breathy mist. The farmer no longer genuflects beside
each muck-shod cow, no practiced hands work milk-bright teats.
Cloistered in their stalls they low, hallowed, overflowing.
Between the pristine snow-globe white outside

and the fertile perfumed gloom locked within, the milk-house
door is the crux to triptych panels of bright and dark —
the way his dying lips are to the wing of living air on one side
and wing of papery breath hauled into watery lung on the other.

His stuttering heart and spittle-caked chin are holy. His grey eyes
are sainted relics pillowed in their sockets. Still weighing him down
in this life, the waning moons of earth under his fingernails are so many
times more blessed than the unction-smeared thumb of the masked priest

who glosses a cross on his forehead, to pronounce him holy
and send him on.

Poems for a Torn Shirt Found in a Tree

I

White litany against thorn, hollow ghost left with only the desire to take
hold, the desert's breath claims you, remakes you, a congregation of one

flayed, laid open, flapping perpetual prayer after prayer
carcass of parchment emptied of belief in an ordinary life

marionette skeleton rearranging itself by the second
pulling your own strings, trying to get comfortable

you're too quick for the tarantula, wasps fill your pocket with paper
hold one part of you whole with purpose while their children grow

a black widow's dream, you web the twigs like a winding sheet
reality has abandoned you and you open your arms

pared down to metaphor your truest heart is poetry
the sun lights you into a piecemeal crescent against the sky

the moon calls you sister, bends to kiss you full of night
the breeze resurrects you, completes you with its fickle flesh

now billowed full, now thin as a rib, you leap back and forth
between the caress of dustdevil and the desolation of forsakenness

sing me the song of forgetfulness, song of shirt-now-something-else,
otherworldly bird fighting for flight against the mesquite

who loves you like a lost kite, so much so you will never go free
doves come to you and mourn their own blue stories in tune

tomorrow tries you on, memory's parched skin worn thin as a secret
you speak from the other side, soul snapping its single note of want

II

This tattered shirt haunting its tree
is my grandmother's ghost bowing
to the wicker basket of sheets
at her feet and rising slowly,
a squat puppet tugged up by the pulley of sun.
With her knobbed hands instinctively
settled on the farthest corners of cotton,
she raises her arms in unconscious
homage to this spring day, then brings
them down with a *snap!* so bright
the whole world answers *amen.*

The twigs that have held the rag of shirt for so long
are worn smooth as the wooden clothespins
she drew in Monday's ceremony from the canvas bag
like all of our names on her rosary,
nouns that pinned down all that's
white with the world.
Five lines of clean percale
holding it all together:
the thread Clotho spins running back
and forth, woven between two poles
rising from shocks of grass
the riding mower could never get
quite close enough to crop. Easter egg
hideouts, snail nests, dinner for deer
and rabbits. So much depended on those
small green blades alive in the wind, waving.

If I Could Only See

—with gratitude for the Webb Space Telescope

Right now, if I could no longer smell or taste
or hear or touch, I would be grateful

for every mote in this shaft of afternoon sun.
Shining rosetta text written in an alphabet where

every letter keeps changing the legend. A rough
map I could read every day despite earthly

distractions: the desire to butter fresh bread,
or to decipher the chirrups of wrens, or to be

warm beneath the bellies of two cats sleeping.
My eyes so finely tuned could witness

every particle's role in the ocean of story
made by our brutal universe's gaudy auras

of explosion and implosion without sound.
How far does light go if it cannot be seen?

Yesterday, I saw a photograph of the youngest
bits of cosmos we have only just begun to glimpse.

And more than once I've lost myself within the
intimate visions of Jupiter and its ribbons of clouds

as they tie and untie their knots around the wild
eyes of hurricane storms that stay or come and go.

This incessant metabolism is creation—hoarding
and releasing, all at once, before and after, for ever

and ever. The very opposite of loss. The inverse of what
I used to feel as a pulse but now know is fertile dust

cycloning in place in the shape of a heart. Gravity loves
attraction and calls it family. A shoal of sunlit fish

like a nebula I could part and dive through, turn back
and look up into. A sky of stars

swimming apart
as I become younger and younger.

Eve to Adam

In the end, it is the teetering forward that matters, the leaning into
what will come despite the sky's clear promise. Only the quickest bones

walk away from their strings. To what end do we press immaculate palms
together if love has coalesced with the grace of woven muscle?

Why should we descend to knee if the staircase looms authentic, the light,
even now, everlasting? And so we crouch at the lip of the ditch and drink.

Water, fickle as the shape of this or any vessel, teaches: be uninhibited
in the seduction of bliss, this fleeting puddle is sacred as anything the cross

will shadow over, ground merely ground, patterns of our feet visiting
fossil tracks, filling steppingstones across it. We heal and

fledge with every reinvention of divinity, and again I am rapt on this verge,
on tiptoe at the latest cliff, balanced above your panic flattened in the grass.

Pressed to the edge, trembling at your private rendering of gravity's
sheer effect, you back away in affirmation of practical equations,

consequences of the speed of falling. Unable to live with the inevitable
bedrock of flesh made dirt, unable to see through to the other side, you

champion the tenuous in the absence of faith. I say: With everything
we need right here in the garden, with nothing we need to pick to fuel

tomorrow's desire, our four hands are free to cup each other.
Let whatever our fingers do not catch when laced together fall away.

The Unmaking

Transfigured by loss
as easy as alchemy
my voice was unmade.

Made up and crowing,
mouth pretentious, pretending,
vows nothing but noise.

Baited with promise,
snared, caged, bitten, the heart starves,
its mouth full of hooks.

Gnawing rumors crack
sugar marrow from branches
in this house of leaves.

Coffined in wet sheets,
wound in outlines not of me,
a bound revenant.

Truth on scratch paper
scrapes the gloss of love to dust,
rasps madness from fact.

Apparitions live
as gristle smeared with lipstick,
choking remainders.

In a rib-caged room
trapped breath heaves, a desperate
wasp at the window.

Chimeras still twitch
between every thing believed
and what is not now.

When what was hidden
slipped, the heart hitched in reflex,
eyelids slit open.

To the Insects

Ancient ones
you still take turns as owners
of the earth
claim daybreak, midday, nightfall
moonlight, rain, mud, snow,
you cling and burrow and fly,
before us
you did not need to learn
any new thing
all was there
in brightness and shadow

You remember
nameless
epochs, geologies, bodies of water
beatings of stars
seasons of planets
the million arcseconds of direction
that point toward shelter, food, drink, warmth
shapes of all the parts of a flower, the ones
that will become fruit and when

You have
your private syllables for coupling,
your own interpretations for
the various kinds of wind

We will talk to you
after there are no animals
say I love you
to the stingered bee, the tiny gnat
those we now crush
in fear or without thought
each a whole being no less than us
heart and belly,
femurs, tibias, eyes and mouth

When we are gone
once again
there will be nothing that's missing
and those of you who can let go
in sleep
when it's time
will awaken with wings

Snakes & Lovers

Tonight's albumen moon is luminous. And so,
in the carnival's glow through our bedroom window,
are your boas. And so is this eye of diamond,
stone on my hand that brims with light
from another side. My finger cool
in its new gold hoop is a river

of flesh in the Tunnel of Love:
one of the only rides going.
This world is all wild night
and lunacy gilded with midway dust scuffed up
by children, carousel lights making moons
of their faces around the caramel-apple
dark of astonished mouths.

We are frenching
in the loom of huge side-show posters, dare
each of those nightmares to watch us in our world.
*See Them Alive! You Won't Believe
Your Eyes!* A two-headed calf jerked

back from the dead. Conjoined triplets
forged at the chest (I imagine one heart
hovering amid three rings of rib). You nuzzle
me against her tattered canvas and I believe
in the Snake Lady's tattooed

scales, earless head, root of tail. Undressed inside
the sawdust fog, we conceive of impossible
infant-sized eggs at her side. Your hands on my hips
convince me of the patron saint of perpetual motion,
friction that conjures unlikely coupling
into sensational child.

Is this why the loss of your snakes'
first clutch surprised us? Eggs of stone,
slick as christmas bulbs nested in a mix
of pine chips, dung, and sloughed-off skin.
A dozen amber globes you lift
into the light, scry like a fortune teller
for a single tiny life.

Love can't help but clutch its tail in its teeth,
heft up its firey self with hope
that something
will jump through.

You toss those ruined jewels
into the trash and I dream

a hundred newborns into bracelets,
each mouth married to its end,
ring upon ring
of iridescent skin
warming on my wrist.

Shell Song

—*for* Chicoreus ramosus, *the branched murex*

Miracle of lace found bright against tidal rocks,
rippled flesh coalesced into stone, you are
the very same crystal as marble, and chalk.
Envy of the glassblower, you mimic the way
the galaxy goes, spines spiral clockwise
around an impossibly miniscule egg,
your years recounted in whorl upon whorl
of serrated ruffle.

Mute tongue torn away, now you sound,
a spiral flute, a skeleton trumpet with sand
for marrow. Mouth of dark, mouth of light,
iridescent lips siren us round the first
blind curve, and so we go,
lost in your hush.

We croon into your cochlear cradle,
sway to the echo in your hollow belly,
the moan of an eons-long poem,
of proteins and calcite and the ache
of a phantom body grieving for
vanished water and salt.

Long ago we blessed you, ate
your body then made you sacred,
a bowl overflowing with the brine of blood,
offerings of gratitude for a living child
or to plead for another successful hunt.

And here you are, heavy in my hand,
extraordinary among ruins heaved
by the power of storm. Tonight,
you are a cupful of rain
under the windless press of Milky Way,
the luminous diatoms in your sky of ocean
replaced by stars.

Sweetgrass

—for Tami Bone

I
In the field across from the stone fence, a child
stomps horse nettle and thistle into a trail
of thorny nests, rubs a pebble in her pocket,
something for her hands to do,
while her eyes try to tease crouched things that shiver
from those that don't.

How can this meadow's secrets be discovered,
flushed, and caught when everything is cloaked
          in dew and breath?
Morning's mist will not be combed into meaning.
She waits.

II
Sunlight separates blades of sweetgrass.
An animal hunkers between escape and stillness.
Where the field ends, a crushed hollow's
cradled hush of shadow
resolves into a velvet shape
so clenched and trembling it shimmers.

Instinct quickens at the juncture of skull
and scapula. Like a hand to the scruff,
fingers of wind lift the quivering fur
          and terrified
the hare bounds up and away and
the child's captive heart leaps after her.

Hall of Fishes

I *Coelacanthus*
> This fish is in shock
> having landed on shore standing up
> while its bones fall down on either side
> of the timeline from fossil to future.
> Rock is no place to swim in.
> Water jangles from its skin
> like coins through fishermen's fingers.
> Here is my hand   holding a lobe
> and we walk.

II *Pygocentrus*
> The placard reads: *A small school*
> *can pick a sheep clean in seconds.*
> Teeth blur until I focus   in slow motion
> a froth of fleece floats up   clouds the water
> the opposite of snow.

III *Otodus megalodon*
> Yawned into a saw-flamed hoop the children
> leap through   the shark jaw.
> A girl snags her hem on a jagged edge
>   as she runs through where the cave
> of stomach was   thread unravels
> backward like the lineage of a mammal.
> Her dress dissolves slowly.

IV *Pleuronectiforms*
> Both flatfish eyes on the starboard side
> are a miracle of metamorphosis.
> One migrates its way through the countries
> of skull   tiny globe of mole groping
> for light on the opposite side
> and the love of its conjoined twin-to-be.
> In one jar, a flounder caught
> with its eye halfway   pearl
> pouched in flesh   I think to myself
> this is as introspective as it gets.

V *Protopterus*
  Earth cut away exposes the African lungfish
  sheathed in seven years of dry sleep
  dreams of me   in this desert
  holding my breath   until the sky
  rains and rains.

Great White

When they winched in the last net
and ran the boards silver with a flood
of herring, no one expected you nested
in the thick of it. To spill out like a ferocious
embryo, flop on the deck adorned in what was
left of the sparkling school, gills emptying
of ocean as you suffocated under the sun.

I am reminded of finding my sister's flipped
goldfish gasping on the carpet under a dying
Christmas tree, like a fallen ornament,
colored lights glancing off its sides,
two brown needles harpooning a delicate fin.

With eighteen feet of teeth and torso
defining a reverent arc around you,
you must have seemed more
thrashing cathedral than landed fish,
as the life leapt out of you
with every jack-knife slap of tail.

The captain kills the crew's visions
of your furious maw insatiable on trophy walls,
commands to toss the whole day's bone-breaking
catch back, fill the holding bin with ocean instead
of ice, and bring you in alive.

You cruise the aquarium of my laptop's tiny screen.
Alone in a voluminous tank, you are a glow
of minnow, an easy target, small as bait.
And then the sliver of diver floats by.

There—in this juxtaposition—is how to
understand why your kind has thrived,
unchanged, the longest on this earth.
The essence of permanence equals simple
efficiency times monstrous consequence.
From the background, the marine biologist's
flat narrative matter-of-factly states
she will not last, says we have not been able
to keep even one of you in a man-made place
for long, and yet we continue
to reel you in, to keep trying.

The Pocket Museum of Natural History

My fingers still expect to feel *something*
each time they fidget with these relics
that mutter in the darkness on my hip.

A small, polished fossil from a lover who dug
deep. Two bones of some animal he knew
I would know. A *Conus textile* shell from the beach
where I was not wanted. A tiny pinecone, forever
closed, hoarding its seedlings. Chip of a painted dish
from a graveyard where we fed none of the dead.

A shard of old purple glass he found in my yard,
rubbed clean with his thumb, now brown with his
blood. Two cherry pits fished from the trash.
A yellow guitar pick I imagined made music for
some other woman. The smoothest pebble from
every place I thought we'd go back to.

I align them all in a different order every time.
Try to read them as an anagram or add on
like an abacus. Try to knot *what once was*
to *all that's left*.

I can't allow these tokens to decompose
into simply shapes or remember meaning
I thought was true and is no longer.
Each remnant still
whispers at the heart's
crossroads of *longing* and *loss,*
of *wish* and *know.*

Is intention severed
at the moment of possession?
Or is there something else
outside the object alive
between the hand that offers
and the palm that wants?
Can the gesture of giving ever solidify?
Or must desire always preserve it
as a gloved ghost of love?

The Loss of Longing

Quick and bright as noon
in this winter desert
I am always awake now
mouth open to a found country
which will never ice over
bones scarred
but no longer wanting.

When the rest of my body
fit into the saguaro's shadow
it turned all the way around
dug in and settled.
Freed of snow
it let go the frozen
casket from its back
empty as expectant sand
and it said *We are home.*

None of these mountains
I see are fences.
All of my kind are here
or arriving, or like me
returning from extinction.
I give my new warm voice
to their chorus.
Hundreds of familiar shapes
some furred, some thorned
some scaled, on hoof and belly
in shells or skin
clouds of wings migrating back.
There is room enough.

No longer needed pieces
of me scorch and crackle
and like sticks gone to ash
are washed away by wind
through a flood-born arroyo.
What remains will be all
that matters, as in these
new seasons I become nothing
but myself, the press of a body
belonging to this earth.

The Last to Know

—*after "Double Major" by Major Jackson*

She emerges whenever I look in the weird mirror, the one
with most of the silver missing, where all I can see are lips
and teeth. If she is only as thin as the foil backing the glass,

then she wonders how heavy her words are. She witnesses
me in the visceral spread of ink on the page and suddenly
believes every line she gives me. Every confession. Every wish.

She doesn't know I'm just a fable in her imagination.
Her other selves are lights floating high up the mountain,
exhausted sightseers with torches, lost in the dark. They are

otherworldly but necessary, and she trusts in them the way
she knows longing and mourning are exactly the same, only buried
in bones of different animals. They point her toward midnight

with a belly full of nightmare. I confuse this with my past
and cannot help her. We've had insomnia for decades.
What she knows that I don't is how to kiss without drowning.

That she doesn't have to be the nail driven into the bedroom
door then hung upon it for later. How to feel an egg is already
an embryo, with a tiny tail and eyes like pearls—a blessed thing

to nurture, not to eat—although she'll never cook for herself.
I'm continually trying to read the signs because there is no way
of telling if what she says about love is true. She calls my fear

of abandonment a sweetness of addiction—like the icing layered
thick on the cakes our grandmother makes, too much is regrettable.
Our voices come together the way two moths mate at dusk, and she

makes me write about this—metaphors for hunger and surrender.
Sometimes behind her eyelids she sees me in the desert,
even though there are spines up close and in all directions.

Often, she wants too much, to be the thorns, the music of pain.
Then I have to pull her out one by one, and every time that
happens, mine is the voice that ends up singing.

The Remaking

Hands entwine to purl
and knit lament into scars.
Knots of heart unsnarl.

Broken curse swallowed,
murmurs of vows dreamed echo
between lips and throat.

Ghost of oath, the tongue
stutters in its shell of teeth,
practicing rapture.

Fossil heart softens
from being to becoming
no longer a cup.

Relic come alive
Clacks as one knuckle resets,
Unbound from its ring.

Throwing off shivers,
the heart ripens with morning,
eats shadows at noon.

Beetles rise in mud
dug fresh from the hollow where
ache was buried, hushed.

The body lets go.
Ripples recast memory
in all directions.

Freed from its bell jar,
the tongue spreads unsalted wings,
fans fire from air, sings.

Love falls to all fours,
immaculate and feral,
sheds loss like rain, runs.

Stones as Indigo as Insomnia

Hunched against the bedroom window, when I whisper, already
asleep, the smoothest of you bangs against the glass, exacts
the same insufferable penance every time I bare my teeth.
No, I won't clatter you across the bedroom floor, make one
more commotion to divine my future. This one I'm in now,
you never saw it coming. Round with smoke and rising, you
camouflage the horizon of my house in stacks I will not climb,
thresholds I will not step over, instead pull apart like warm
bread I butter and gnaw when there is no kindling to gather.
When the largest of you ripens, the flesh will be a confession
too heavy to harvest, a weight in my lap, rooting down. You are
fists without the knucklebones I've shattered having beaten
against the porcelain breast of memory. Crowd my hands,
leave no room to hold the sweated salt of another's, no inch
of fresh air for a skinned heartline to breathe in. To let go,
if I tried, I would rage you at the recurring purgatory I reach for
every time my palms wake up empty.

Fleshed in Stone

—regarding Archaeopteryx lithographica

Broken sparrow, caught in this mud-bogged field,
clover pressed within the frames of your tangled
wings, crooked feet, open beak empty of song,

the drying earth cuddled and loved you month
after month, to the moment I discovered white
bones haloed with the ghosts of feathers,

and dug you out. What a reincarnation you
are, an homage to twisted *Archaeopteryx*, an
ossified child of a fossilized phenomenon.

Your kindred rush to save you late at night,
fly at my lighted window again and again,
imprint the glass with wingspans smashed

open like maps where roadway bones
show up in x-ray, lit with morning sun. Exactly
like this tender fossil captive on a postcard

from Chicago: the only Cretaceous
vertebrate to wing all the way to today. Its
feathers carry on in offspring, crow, ibis, owl,

fall like leaves from dodo, snowy egret, crane,
and condor. O rock of ages, you're on the move,
fleshed out in stone. Head thrown back, wishbone

hurtling ever forward, your claw-fingered wings leap
the lizard gap to songbird, your feet reach out
to grasp my fingers just below the paper's edge.

Hyena Queen

—for Julie Speed

I'm sick of chucking sticks for this pack
of lip-lickers.
I've thrown
my last bone yet still they skulk
at the hem of my skirt, lurk
in the twilight of my afternoon shadow.
Lovers, of course, are deterred
by all this blood. Except by muzzles,
my underbelly goes
un-nuzzled. All my shoes are ruined.
Was it just last March I decided
I looked sharp in bite marks?
Now I long for a single nipless
kiss. To spoon without scruff
up my nose. A bed clean of femurs
and leftovers. Lettuce.

In the beginning, I couldn't resist
all the bows and crouching, this
congregation lit with smirks and
swift with hot gifts, their croons day
and night sweet like clockwork.
With never a lack for lunch
or lullabies, a girl could grow
attached to this lathe of cave,
loll stinking in its grip for days,
dosed on liver. My mother's
mother had a taste
for sweetbreads. I, too, know
to be thrilled by gizzards piled
fresh at my feet. More than enough
is finally too much.
Have I forgotten the sun,
the laundered scent of sky,
the crisp silence behind
this cult of flies? Time to stand up,
shake them off.
Make a break for the trees.

Beatifying the Animals

—for Julie Speed

Once dewclaw accumulated into opposable thumb,
how could we not begin to gesture?
Like deluded prestidigitators, we believe a sign
of the cross etched mid-air conjures
just as solidly as a single digit sawed across
the throat. We bang the gavel because
it has a handle. We classify. We relegate.
Unlike the hound, unlike the heifer, we can finger
the equal number of letters
in *salvation* and *slaughter,*
point with parallel dexterity
toward the davenport and the abattoir.
Our thumbs go up.
Our thumbs come down.

When sitting in barcalounger judgment
with the footrest flipped up, determination
is easy to swallow if interpreted in terms
of appendage: *Whoever holds the salt
shaker wins.* Our souls' evolution reverses
in the parabola of t-bone tossed from fist
to dog-jaw. *I fling, therefore I am.*
Soon we are apes saying it.

And who can blame us
for not beatifying the animals?
If we toss out the cow heart that could not
muscle us to love it,
wave away the backyard mutt
congealed to tow chain discarded
like the mangy couch she's bound to,
then we are free to walk the staircase
up to heaven on our hands.

This Nothing Is Not Darkness

*To become a butterfly, a caterpillar inside a chrysalis must first
digest itself.*
                    —Scientific American

I carry a secret
The terrible voice of a god
Inside my mouth
Compels me
No above or below
I know only this leaf
And the next and then
Leaf after leaf after leaf after leaf
Hunger so erotic it is
All there is
Whet by dread
There will never be enough

This relentless effort to live
Is to grow and split
Grow and split
Over and over and finally

Dangle from the voice of a god
Between cloud and earth
I carry a secret
My skin whines with intention
Splits for the last time
Reveals
Me unseen in a casket

I tremble with
This instinct
To decompose
Consume every
Thing I am
From the inside out

What is real when there are
No more eyes to know?
What is truth at the moment of
Absolute dissolution?
This nothing is not darkness

I carry a secret
The ruthless voice of a god
That made me
Unmakes me
Into an inferno of stars where
Every cell is singing

What is almost impossible is

Wings rise to the surface
The world clears and
Faceted eyes refract
The elemental light
Now wholly new

I'm breathing in lucidity

Escaping the branch
And its green addiction
I carry a secret
The throbbing voice of a god
In my reborn belly is a beggar
Obsessed by color
Starved for sweetness
Delirious with need
For a fragile
Incandescent lover

Endling

—for Lonesome George, the last known member of the species
Achatinella apexfulva.

Hallowed be the name
of this snail, the texture of it
a whorl of thirst in my throat.
Along this branch lives
the absence of iridescent evidence
of how it emerged, lengthened
yearned
for a future it will never stretch to.

Why do we say "*went*" extinct
as if the very last
dried specimen frictioned back
to yesterday—maybe stepped out
for a walk—and might return at any moment
pregnant and glistening?

The genetic gift of flesh
that grew inside
a spiral lamp like a djinn
is now not even a seed of dust.
The holy place is shuttered.

For fourteen years
this lonley snail's love
darts meant for a mate
punctured loss in a glass
garden. Like a period
at the end of an eon's song
its final arrow
carried story and chords and spaces
that came before it.
Nothing after unless
a resurrection.

The law of entropy drags
everything to dissolution
eventually, especially
that which is most tender.

A lesson my heart has yet to learn
as it chants along to
its own solitary throb
snug in a wet bone shell.

Playing with Gravity

There is no way of knowing
What I tell you about love is true.
Go by the signs.
　　　　　—Frank Stanford

Set these on my altar:
eggs of desert quail
in rows across from
sun-bleached shells.
Abandoned things
saved from the ground.
Enough for chess.
Quickening
golden yolks
opposed by
beautiful ruins.
Lowing hearts and
hollowed bellies
lean in the direction
of each other,
trade places.

These moves are sewn
together with gravity,
like the moon
towing at blood
then letting go,
or the bodies
of planets,
elliptical and silent
in their orbits,
straining to escape until
the groaning knots
are pulled undone.

This is how you learn
the syzygy of love and loss
and longing: like an echo
commanded by a shout,
give in unconditionally
when carried away
by the opposition.

Notes

Page 1 [Confession of a Lepidopterist] With a wingspan of 4.5 to 5 inches, *Actias luna*, the nocturnal luna moth, is one of the largest of the family *Saturniidae* in North America. Emerging from the cocoon without a mouth, it never feeds as an adult; its sole purpose is to mate and reproduce within a one-week lifespan.

Page 2 [Bee Litany] Saint Ambrose (339-397 CE), "the honey tongued doctor," has as his emblem the beehive, symbolizing his eloquence as a preacher and a teacher. According to legend, he was unharmed when, as a child, a swarm of bees settled on him. —*Saints: Who They Are and How They Help You* by Elizabeth Hallam

Page 4 [Wunderkammer] is German for "room of wonder," i.e. one of the cabinets of curiosities that emerged in Europe in the sixteenth century as forebears of the natural history museum. "The great embalmers and preparators kept their ingredients secret, but Ruysch apparently used some combination of wax, resin, talcum, and cinnabar pigment. The injected fluid had to perfuse all the vessels without rupturing them, and then harden only after filling the complete system." —*Finders, Keepers: Treasures and Oddities of Natural History* by Stephen Jay Gould

Page 16 [Sweetgrass] was inspired by Tami Bone's photograph that came to be named after the poem. www.tamibone.com

Page 17 [Hall of Fishes] The coelacanth is a fossil lobed fish regarded as ancestral to amphibians and other land vertebrates. Long thought to be extinct since the Cretaceous, one was discovered to be living off the coast of South Africa in 1938, and several more have been observed and/or caught since. It's listed as critically endangered and commands a high price on the black market.

Page 25 [Fleshed in Stone] "*Archaeopteryx lithographica* ('ancient wing imprinted in stone' in Greek) was a genus of small, bird-like dinosaurs from the late Jurassic in what is now Europe. Widely recognized as the earliest known bird... it cut a starkly contrasting image, boasting a snout filled with sharp teeth, wings with claws and a long, bony tail. Despite [this], it shares many similarities with modern avians: a small size, a wishbone and asymmetrical feathers, to name a few." —*Smithsonian Magazine*

Page 26 [Hyena Queen] was inspired by Julie Speed's painting *Vito and the Hyena Queen*. www.juliespeed.com

Page 27 [Beatifying the Animals] "A couple of times a year a church lady would come and try to convince us to join her religion, which said that only 144,000 souls would be allowed into heaven.... I asked her what about the souls of animals, and she answered without even a hint of doubt that she was quite sure they never went to heaven." —Julie Speed, on painting *The Intercession*, from *Queen of My Room*.

Page 28 [This Nothing Is Not Darkness] was inspired by the metamorphosis of the luna moth, *Actias luna*. "To become a butterfly, a caterpillar inside a chrysalis must first digest itself. Then certain groups of cells turn the soup into eyes, wings, antennae, legs, genitals, and all the other adult structures." —*Scientific American* [see "Confession of a Lepidopterist"]

Page 30 [Endling] is the term used by scientists to refer to the final living member of a species. Lonesome George was the last yellow-tipped O'ahu tree snail *Achatinella apexfulva*, which went extinct on January 1, 2019. George was born in a captive breeding facility... in the early 2000s, and the rest of its kin died soon after. From 2016 on, it lived alone in a laboratory terrarium at the University of Hawaii outside of Kailua, O'ahu. Although these snails are hermaphrodites, two adults must mate to produce offspring, stimulating each other with tiny "love darts." Named after the Pinta Island tortoise in the Galapagos who was also the last of his kind, the snail lived to be fourteen years old. Its DNA has been preserved for possible cloning in the future. —source: *National Geographic*

Michele M Miller has worked as a copywriter and senior editor, a director of marketing and public relations, a book, exhibition, and publication designer, an assistant photography curator, and as event manager and marketer of visiting writer readings for the creative writing program at Texas State University in San Marcos. She holds an MFA in creative writing from the University of Arizona. Prizes awarded for her poetry include an Arizona Commission on the Arts fellowship, and her thesis manuscript, "The Cinderella Heart," was runner-up for the National Poetry Series, and the Kore Press First Book Prize. Michele writes and photographs in her heartland, the Sonora desert of Tucson, Arizona.